Make it Rain:
The Secret to Generating Massive Paydays from Your Email List

Chris Orzechowski

Make it Rain:

Copyright © 2019, Chris Orzechowski

Published in the United States of America

181119-01239-2

ISBN: 9781094709666
Independently published

No parts of this publication may be reproduced without correct attribution to the author of this book.
For more information on 90-Minute Books including finding out how you can publish your own book, visit 90minutebooks.com or call (863) 318-046

Here's What's Inside...

Introduction.. 1

How to Make It Rain.. 7

How to Make a Boatload of Sales Every
Time You Email Your List....................................... 9

First Pillar:
Three Types of Email Campaigns 14

Second Pillar:
Every Thing is Personality-Based 24

Third Pillar:
Selling With Stories 33

Fourth Pillar:
Smart Segmenting... 39

Fifth Pillar:
Your Central Theme.. 48

Increase Amount of Sales That
You're Currently Making from Your
Email Marketing 51

Introduction

In my work as a copywriter, I realized there is great power in having an email list, and in learning how to build a relationship with people by effectively communicating with them through an email list. I saw a lot of power in doing this with all of my clients who had big lists, but it wasn't until I started building *my* own list that I truly understood how powerful this can be.

My own business was at a point where I was working with a lot of clients but without a lot of leverage. I didn't have any way of earning revenue unless my butt was physically on the seat, doing all the writing work myself. After I started to build my email list and sell products, things started to take off, because I had leveraged income. Since I wasn't working with as many people on a one-to-one basis anymore, I was able to build some scale into what I was doing.

A while back, I was in the middle of doing a lot of back-to-back launches for my clients. My list on the side had grown to 273 subscribers, so one day I decided to take a little break from all the launches and send one email to my list, which generated $1,720 in affiliate commissions. I said to myself: "Wow, I should probably do more of this because it makes a lot more sense." It was a lot easier than doing one-on-one work, and it showed me how powerful emails could be.

For every business that gets good at email communication, they have a license to print money.

Whether you have a large or a small list, if it is actively growing and you have good offers, it's incredibly easy to sell, because the people on that list chose to be there. It's not like trying to advertise to a cold audience on Facebook, which is also part of the equation, but the people on your email list will be your best people... the people who love your stuff.

With the amount of time it takes to write a simple little email, there's so much leverage. It's such an easy, lucrative opportunity for any business.

Is Email Taking its Last Gasping Breath?

Everyone says, "Email is dead, it's dying across the industry," but in my opinion, it's getting more and more important. There are more email service providers, email solutions, and software options than ever. People are checking emails more often than they ever have before. By the numbers, more sales are made through email than ever before. It's getting a little bit tougher to say 'email is dead.'

If you review raw data from companies and compare baseline open rates and baseline click-through rates, sure, responses might have slowed down a bit. The main reason is because most of these companies suck at email. Think about it this way: you still need an email address to do anything online. That's the beginning of your identity online.

What happened is that many companies never adapted their strategies. It doesn't work the way it did in 2004 anymore, when you could still make a killing blasting out any random offer via email. Everyone used to love getting an email and you could send whatever you wanted, but the game has changed... and that's a good thing. You must change your strategy to be one of those people whose emails get consumed, to avoid blending in with all the noise of what everyone else is doing.

I hope this book inspires you to realize that if you have an email list, it doesn't matter if you have 100 people or 100,000. You are probably sitting on a profitable gold mine in your business.

If you start implementing this simple email strategy from this book, you will have the ability to make sales on command, and generate massive paydays for yourself. It will transform your business completely.

Failing to Leverage the Email List

A lot of companies leave big money on the table by failing to leverage their email list because they don't know what to do. There are a lot of course creators, coaches, consultants, bloggers, e-commerce store owners, SaaS and tech companies and people who have been told for years, *"Build your list. Build your list."* That takes a lot of focus, and that's important advice (you should always be building your list), but then they say, "Once I build a list I'll figure out what to do later," and they never figure it out. Many people lack strategy.

Some people don't know what to write, and they're afraid that if they send something, the whole list will unsubscribe. "I'll go from 50,000 down to zero if I send a bad email." (This is kind of ridiculous - that's never going to happen.)

Maybe they are sending emails without getting any response, so they say, *"Well, we tried that a few times and it didn't work."*

Confusion 101

These are all valid reasons; I understand why this happens. Sometimes you might be sitting at the screen, not sure what to write. You don't know what to type into the subject line, or you've sent a few emails that no one's opened, or the people who have opened haven't clicked through, so you haven't made any sales. It gets frustrating. Maybe they have opened and clicked an email, but no one's bought. You are still spending all this money on email software and building your list, but it's not working. It seems like when you look at your inbox, everyone is doing something different. How do you know what's right to do for your business?

A big part of the problem is the lack of a predictable process for getting people to buy their products through the emails they send. People get frustrated because they see all these other businesses making email work, but they don't know how to do it; maybe they think their list is too small, and they need 500,000 or a million subscribers before they can start making sales.

Some people might think it will take forever or that once they hit a certain number, they can start selling to their list. But the fact remains that I've been able to make sales to my list with a few hundred people, and I'm no one special. It's a matter of implementing the right strategy and putting it to work for you, and buying in.

The good thing about what I teach is that it's not overwhelming. It's fairly easy to pick up and learn, and easy to stick with. Once you see the results, you will want to stick with it.

How to Make It Rain

When you add a solid email marketing strategy into your business, everything starts to change. You will never, ever have to worry about where your sales are coming from because you will have automated systems in place that let you make sales almost every single day, if not every single day; these systems will include following up with all the segments of your list. If the segments are set up right, you will also have the ability to make sales on command. Any time you want to generate some sales, you will have the power to say, "Hey, I'd like to make some money today." Then you send out an email to your list, and all you have to do is collect the cash. That's an awesome feeling.

Your business model also gets very simple. So many entrepreneurs are trying to do a million different things, and they can make online marketing incredibly complex. I have worked on funnels with 20 videos, hundreds of emails, and

20 different ads on the front end (on Facebook, Google, and everywhere else). You can make some crazy funnels, or simplify things to reach the point where the main drivers in your business are getting people onto your email list, and then selling them stuff. If you can accomplish growing your list and increasing your sales, you can make your business easy and fun to run.

Also, building your list will give you a lot of leverage, *because it takes the same amount of time to send an email to one person as it takes to send an email to 100,000 people.* It doesn't take you any longer to write that email, whether it takes you 10 minutes or half an hour. The larger your list, the better your offer; also, the better relationship you have with your list, the more money you will make. But the amount of time it takes to write that email doesn't necessarily change, so you get extreme leverage.

How to Make a Boatload of Sales Every Time You Email Your List

Keep it Simple = Easy Sales

If you can type words into a box, and hit a send button, you can make this work. It's not like you need some crazy, super complex coding skills. Soon we'll review the content of what goes into an email, but it's super low-tech and super simple; you don't necessarily have to be a trained writer or copywriter to make this work, because email copy is conversational, and it sounds the same way that you talk. Many of these email software packages are very user-friendly, so everything you're doing is simplified.

As your business gets simplified, your daily schedule gets simplified. Once I started focusing on marketing to my email list, as the main thing to do daily (or a few times a week), I needed to make sure that emails went out. If that was happening, money was coming into my business, which removed a lot of stress from the equation of everything I was trying to do. When people start loving your stuff, a lot of new opportunities start to emerge.

Recently, when I sent an email to my list, someone read a piece of my content and invited me onto their podcast. Being a podcast guest positions you as a content creator who is adding to the conversation. It builds a strong bond. You turn people into raving fans instead of random people on the list.

You start to build an audience, a following, a tribe, all of which goes back to that Kevin Kelly article, *1,000 True Fans*. Email is the medium that builds or attracts those 1,000 true fans. They might see some of your content online, such as your videos or interviews or ads, but the relationship is built through email.

Once you become good at this, people start to love reading your emails. They look forward to your emails; they start responding and forwarding them to their friends. They buy from these emails. It becomes a habit for them, and it makes selling so much easier to this warm audience (instead of a cold audience).

I've even had people on my list reach out and ask about future courses. *"Can I get first in line? How much will it be? I want to start saving money so I can buy it in a month."* They don't even know what it is yet, but they ask because I've established that bond with my list. Anyone can do that with their lists.

When you get good at email, everything in your business and your life gets so much easier. You don't have to run around spending a ton of money on website traffic just to make sales. I still recommend spending money to grow your list but, it gets a lot simpler. These objectives become the focus of your business: grow your list, send emails that make people like you, and make people want to buy your stuff.

Many people have written off email; they probably aren't putting in a lot of energy, time, or thought into the emails that they send. When it's done well, people don't feel like they are being sold to. They feel connected with the person sending the emails, someone they look forward to hearing from. Consumers sometimes have a negative feeling about typical sales emails, but there's a reason for that. It's because people don't want to read ads in their inbox. That's just the way it is.

Types of Emails

People get two kinds of emails. Some communications are a bit more personal, and some are blatant advertisements. I get emails daily from some big apparel companies; about six times a day. Every email says something like this: "50% off sale", with a picture of what they want me to buy. You eventually just learn to tune out and delete them.

I've seen this with a software company who's list I'm on, which has literally sent me the exact same email about 20 days in a row. I'm not even joking. It's the same subject line, the same body copy, and the same images as the email to get me to sign up for their service. I do not understand this strategy at all. Why would they think that works? If I didn't respond to the first 19 duplicate emails, why would they think that am I really going to respond the 20th time?

The crazy thing is and despite their awful strategy, they still make sales! Another thing to remember is this simple fact: companies wouldn't be sending so many emails if they didn't work. And while bigger companies can make up for lackluster strategy, if you have a smaller business... you have to play the game a little differently.

For instance, if you sell courses, and you don't have millions of people on your list, then you have to play a bit of a different game than just sending out blatant ads. You can't play the big companies' war of attrition by playing the numbers game, hoping to convert as many possible subscribers into buyers. It's not going to work as well for you. So, let me tell you what WILL work. I use a set of Core Pillars as my strategy.

First Pillar: Three Types of Email Campaigns

Every one of these campaigns will have a very specific objective. I call them 'campaigns', because if you were going into a battle or war, you would always have an objective. There are three kinds of sequences that I like to use for all my clients and my own business.

1. Autoresponder sequences
2. Broadcast sequences
3. Launch sequences

Autoresponder Sequence Campaigns

First, an autoresponder sequence is something that every business should have. Some businesses have multiple autoresponder email sequences; these sequences are triggered to send out something when a new person signs up to your list. Now, most business should have a welcome sequence. As soon as someone signs up, they will get a drip sequence of emails letting them know all about the company, what's in it for them, and all the cool stuff that will be coming their way.

I like to start these autoresponder sequences with a combination of stories, like the creation story of the product or the company, because that starts to build the bond. I like to tell stories about how this company is different, how the products are different, and why our products are superior.

It's not necessarily all about the company itself. I've done this for one of my clients who sold watches. "This is our mission, why we started this company, and why we are offering these limited-edition, luxury, Italian-handcrafted timepieces for a fraction of the price. This is our big why." People understood the message, "We are not some other company trying to sell you something. We have a mission and we'd like you to join us." We do all these things to build a bond between the reader and the products we are trying to sell in our company, in our brand.

Another email in this company's autoresponder sequence was a story about how you get ripped off every time you buy a watch from a mall department store, because of the huge markups. That's something we stand against.

In these main autoresponders, when someone is joining your list, you have an opportunity to tell a lot of these stories. If you've ever read any Seth Godin works, especially his book *All Marketers Are Liars*, he talks about the importance of story: *"Everyone is telling themselves a story about your product or your business."* The autoresponder sequence, when someone signs up, is a great place to start building that bond, telling the stories that you would like people to identify with your company.

The cool part about the main autoresponder sequence is that you can convert subscribers into buyers very quickly. You will be able to identify all of the hyper-buyers, the people who are ready to buy right away. In my own business, I set up a great autoresponder; it was great because I wrote it one time, and then it ran in the background for months and months without me having to do a thing. As people signed up to my list, content dripped out to them day after day. I made some soft pitches in that autoresponder sequence; people were reaching out to me, interested in hiring me, and I didn't have to do anything. Honestly, all I did was find a way to build my list. I knew the emails were going out. I didn't have to touch anything. It was a completely hands-off process.

But we don't only want to do that one thing; that's just the first part of the strategy. Depending on how people get into your funnel, it could be coming in through a webinar or a product launch; they could be signing up on your website, or you could be giving them a book or a lead magnet, or something else. You will always want to have some automated sequence to begin that conversation with those prospects, to start bonding with them by demonstrating value. One thing that is so important about this overall strategy is this idea:

"Make your emails valuable."

Making your emails look inherently valuable doesn't necessarily mean you have to give away a ton of content, and tell them how to do this or that. If someone pays $20 at the theater for a movie ticket, they got value because they were entertained, not because of an ROI on their purchase or anything like that. People derive and define value differently from different buying experiences. The autoresponder is your first opportunity to begin building that value and trust with the subscriber, building that bond, and also identifying and converting those people who are ready to buy right now.

These things are great because they do the selling for you. You set them up once, monitor them to make sure they are doing well and over time, make any necessary improvements.

Broadcast Sequence Campaigns

Second, the cool thing about the broadcast sequence campaign is that it's ongoing. As you are doing things in your business, as you work with clients and hear success stories, this is your opportunity to infuse all of these things into your broadcast sequence; it's almost like the show *Flip or Flop*, one of those HGTV house-flipping shows that my wife and I watch all the time. Tarek and Christina, the two hosts, flip houses for a living; obviously they're making money while they're doing that work, but I started to realize their strategy.

They were doing the work once but getting paid twice; first they did the work of the actual thing they do, and then they were getting paid to talk about it.

It doesn't matter what you sell. Even if you sell an e-commerce product or a software program, you will be working with customers, helping them get specific results or outcomes, so you are already getting paid to do that work.

When you can talk about it and turn it into your email broadcast series - called a 'broadcast' because it's almost like your personal reality TV show - you let people know about all the good work that you are doing with others. You are sharing the success stories and telling cautionary tales, so people don't fall into the same mistakes.

In your broadcast sequence, you are selling the entire time. It's not like pitching or saying, *"Hey, buy my thing,"* over and over. You are doing a lot of demonstration using stories.

This is one example of a very simple broadcast email that I use all the time with my email list. I'll say, "I've started working with this writer; they were struggling with X, and I told them to do Y, and this was the result. If you'd like to get the same results, here's how we can work together; click here and get started."

People can quickly get tired of emails. But if they are interested in your content, and the stories that you tell, and all the cool things you are doing in your life or even in the day-to-day happenings at your company, then you can make a very effective broadcast sequence and sell a lot of products.

You'll never run out of content because you are always doing things in your life.

You are always working with more people. That ongoing sequence doesn't necessarily have a start date and an end date. You start it up, and you never stop. The cool thing is that the sequence can make sales for you. Any time something cool happens, you can update people on your list by sending an email and make sales.

Some people choose to do this every single day. I don't think you need to necessarily, although if you are making sales every single time you send an email, you might want to start. I don't always email every day. Some weeks I do and some I don't, but it can be very effective.

Launch Sequence Campaigns

The third campaign is the launch sequence, which is like a broadcast but with a very definite time limit. Maybe you are promoting an affiliate's product, or holding a special class or a workshop. Maybe you have a limited amount of inventory so you are launching a product to generate a lot of cash, to generate a big payday for yourself in a short amount of time. For some clients, we helped them create a few emails that made more sales in a seven-day period than they had made in a seven-month period, which is pretty crazy. You get extreme leverage with launches because they are deadline-driven; there's a lot of urgency behind these campaigns.

Some people don't like to use launches at all, and that's fine. But there are always certain things that you will do in your business that have associated deadlines. For an e-commerce store, you might have a limited release, or you're releasing a product for the first time, or you are having a special sale. Those launches will be effective.

If you are selling information as a coach or doing some live event, you will have some limits or a deadline when people need to respond by a certain date. Putting those elements in place will give you the ability to generate big paydays for yourself.

Examples

To demonstrate the power, I'll unpack the process and show you how we used all three of these sequences interchangeably, within one cohesive system.

One of my clients was a personal finance blogger, and another was a Facebook Ads agency owner; these two clients teamed up and created a business selling courses that helped people use Facebook Ads as a 'side hustle.' They also created another course about how bloggers can use Facebook Ads. I worked with them to help nail down their email marketing strategy, because when they first began, they had a lot of subscribers on an email list but they weren't leveraging it. They were both growing their lists and making a decent amount of money, but once I helped them get set up with an email strategy, it was like throwing gasoline on the fire.

Since they were launching a new product, the first thing we did was to run a launch sequence on their list. That launch sequence generated $139,000 in four days, which is pretty good, because previously they were doing about $15,000 a month. It was a nice little bump from that one revenue event. You could see why there was so much leverage; it was a very tight four-day window to open up the cart and accept sales, but we were able to create a great result.

About six weeks later, we relaunched that product and did another $100,000. Then we took the entire launch sequence, and with very slight edits, made it evergreen. We turned it into an automated sequence.

One of the other reasons why I wanted to write this book was from a conversation with a client about a very simple, twelve-email sequence I set up for their business. This client had been traveling for a while; I asked him, *"Hey, how's the business going?"* He said, *"Oh, man. I haven't done anything in about six weeks. I checked the dashboard, and we made $35,000 last month in sales."* I said, *"Wow, that's pretty good for not doing anything for over a month."*

That's the power of having solid automated sequences working for you in the background at all times, bringing you customers, bringing you sales. We didn't need 100 emails to get this result. We used solid copy and a well-structured sequence to make that happen.

After those automated sequences have been set up, they'll periodically do launch sequences; in between, they'll do broadcasts a few times every week to their lists, sometimes five times depending on what they are offering. Sometimes it's content; often it's a product promotion, or sometimes they'll promote other people's products. Using all three of these campaigns interchangeably has transformed their business, and at this point they're knocking on the door of a million dollars in their first 12 months.

I don't know if they will hit it in 12 months, but a lot of that was done with good copy, good email sequences, good products, and an incredible list. They do a good job building their community and everything else, but if you have those elements in place, it could really transform everything you are doing.

Second Pillar: Every Thing is Personality-Based

This is something important: People are starting to bond with personalities. If you look at fast-food companies like Wendy's, McDonald's, and Burger King, they don't necessarily communicate as big corporate entities. If you look at Wendy's Twitter account, they are talking smack about Burger King, Sonic, and all these other food chains. It's funny. It's like a real person is writing it, and people are starting to identify with these "corporate personalities."

From Human to Human

Even when individuals follow the news, they'll probably follow their favorite news anchor or news sources on Twitter for their take on all of these issues. We are starting to move into a world that's all about the personal brand. Even big companies have spokespeople, because it helps people form a bond with the company.

I've seen some companies with a huge list; they'll send out pitches and promote someone else's offer, or someone will buy an email drop to their list, or they'll send a blatant advertorial piece of copy to their list, hoping to generate a lot of sales. That worked for a while, but I don't know if that's working as well anymore. The clients who do the best are personality-based in their email, meaning they talk like one human to another human. It seems obvious, but a lot of people mess this up.

Make sure that your emails are as close to a one-to-one communication as possible, because people want to read emails from a friend they enjoy hearing from, a person that they know, like, and trust. Remember, it all goes back to people not wanting ads in their inbox. We have enough of that.

Some services will help you mass-unsubscribe from lists because people are sick and tired of all these ads they don't want. I'm not saying that they necessarily want a ton of content either, so there's a little bit of a fine line. But people get on your list because they have problems; one reason why they are on the list is because they think you can help them get a specific result in their life.

They do want to buy something. They know (deep down in their heart) that's why they are there in the first place, but they also want to be entertained. They also want to build a bond and have that relationship with you. They want all of these things to happen, but that won't happen if you are speaking like a corporate entity. Make your speech one-to-one, because they are reading it as one person, not as an audience of people. One person reads the email.

One of my clients has been in the online marketing space for over 20 years. He's done an incredible job with his emails; they have a personal touch that a lot of people are missing. Every email is story-based, and includes stories from his life. I'm always telling stories from my life in emails, telling stories about the work I do with clients, and the work that I do with the people that I coach. I'm making observations about things that I see in the marketplace.

It's all about the personal brand. It's not like, *"Hey, I've got this product, buy it here."* A lot of people make these mistakes, but you must infuse some of your life into your email; if you don't want to do that, find someone who can infuse the life of the brand into the emails.

When you look at a company like Dollar Shave Club, they have a certain style, a specific voice. They have a sense of humor with their writing. It's not stiff and corporate. There is some personality behind what they were doing, which is super, super important. Everything you do in email has to be personality-based.

On the following pages, there is an example of what I mean by personality-based email. The example is an email I sent to my list, selling tickets for a copywriting event where I was speaking.

==================================

Subject: *How to become an instant authority*

So a few months ago, I did something that really helped me stand out from a lot of my competitors.

I was kind of scared to do it. But I'm really glad I made it happen.

The cool thing is... it's something anyone can do. And when you do it, you'll instantly be seen as an authority... and it'll become a whole heck of a lot easier to "sell YOU", get more clients, grow your list, and grow your business.

I'm talking, of course, about speaking at events.

I got an email a few days ago from a subscriber who was wrestling with the decision about whether or not he should give a speech to a group of business owners. He told me that he was a little scared to get on stage.

He asked me whether he should go through with it or not. So I told him...

"DO IT!"

I wrote an article all about my experience on stage, for the first time. ***(You should click here and read it.)***

Before that speech...

I was never on stage before. The biggest audience I'd ever spoken to was a classroom full of 12 kids who didn't want to be there. But when I got the invite, there was no way I was saying no.

Once you step on stage one time... congratulations - you're now a speaker.

You literally give speeches to groups of people industry. It's an instant authority builder. And it's something I highly recommend.

In fact, even if you can't get on stage just yet... just showing up to a live event will make a huge difference in your career. You never know who you're going to meet.

When I went to Affiliate Summit East a few years back, I didn't know anyone at all in the industry... let alone anyone who would be there at that event.

As I was sitting in the room for the "welcome" session for first timers, a man and his wife sat down right in front of me. And I recognized this guy.

It was Gary Bencivenga.

I ended up having a conversation with him and his wife, and he gave me some really awesome advice. That wouldn't have happened if I just stayed home.

The last event I went to was a dinner, where I found myself with a bunch of people who are "celebrities" in our industry. People you can't just call up and take out for a meal.

Amazing things can happen when you go to live events.

You can meet clients. You can learn some cool stuff. But more importantly... you make relationships with people.

It's a lot easier for someone to send you clients or make an intro or wanna do a JV if you've shaken their hand before... and had a chance to look em in the eye.

And I know there are a LOT of big events out there. Most people wanna go to some of these big industry events where there's thousands of people in the room.

Me? I don't go to those big events. I prefer small, intimate gatherings with high-level people. I like speaking at and attending events where there are only a hundred or so people in the room. Because that's where career-changing introductions are made.

Now, there's one event I think you should really consider going to.

It's called The Copywriter Club In Real Life. It's happening in Brooklyn in about a month. I will be speaking there. And I'm giving a brand new talk with my partner in crime, Kim Krause Schwalm. It's going to be awesome, I promise you that. I want you to come and join me. And I'll even take you out to lunch if you buy a ticket through my super special affiliate link. Here it is:

Click here to get your ticket for The Copywriter Club In Real Life

They've just updated the sales page and elaborated a little more about all the awesome things that are happening at this year's event.

But know this...

They are raising the prices of tickets VERY soon. And being that the room is limited, and they've been promoting it a lot... I am not sure how much longer tickets are going to be available.

This is one of the few events that's catered specifically to Copywriters. So make sure you grab your ticket today.

See you there,

Chris Orzechowski

P.S. Am I going to see you there? Reply back and let me know...

==================

Watch and Learn

So, contrast this email with most of the emails you see in your inbox.

Most of them will say "50% off... sale ending soon..." Essentially, it's "buy my stuff"!

Would you rather get emails like that, where they just try to ram a sale down your throat... or do you think using some 'reason why' copy and injecting some personality might make your readers actually look forward to the emails you're sending?

Obviously, this email example is a little longer than yours have to be. But take a look at how I injected my personality into this, instead of sounding cold, stiff and corporate.

Make it Fun

One of my clients, Jeff Walker, emails a lot of stories about things that have happened to him in business, or lessons that he's learned. As his business evolved, the emails explained mistakes that he's made, or why he's had the successes that he's had. It's a common theme with all the people who do great with email.

One of my clients was this company called Chef'd, a pretty big meal delivery company. We didn't say, "Hey, buy our food." We said, "We are going to tell you this cool story about something we're doing."

Every time we had a promotion, there was always some story with a personality behind it. We spoke in a specific way. We had a voice to the brand. A lot of people neglect these things that are very, very important. They send corporate and dry content, that's stuffy and not interesting to read. It's not fun or entertaining to read. Infusing that personality into the content is important.

Third Pillar: Selling With Stories

I know I've touched on this before, but you will use stories in every one of your campaigns, whether it's a launch, an autoresponder, or a broadcast series. That's because stories are demonstrative by nature. That's why parables and fairy tales exist, and why we remember Disney movies instead of things we read in a textbook in school, because the stories impart lessons to us. We always tell stories, because stories stick out in our mind, and they are easy to recite back to other people. For thousands of years, that's been the main method of transmitting lessons and information from one person to another.

Stories are Sticky

For instance, maybe I say, *"Hey, you should probably stop smoking, because it's probably not good for you."* There's a good chance you'll brush off that advice, because people are stubborn and we don't like being told what to do. That's part of human nature. But if I tell you a story about my cousin whose teeth started rotting to the point where they all fell out... and died a year later, you might say, *"Holy crap, I'm going to stop smoking."*

That's a very sad and graphic (made up) example, but which one of those pieces of advice sticks with you more? The second makes it more human, brings it down to earth. It's not some pie-in-the-sky advice. The latter example is a lot more demonstrative, and a lot more powerful in communicating your ideas through a story.

There are all kinds of stories you could use, from clients' stories to personal stories from your own life. You could use cautionary tales or stories from history. I have a buddy named Sean Mysel, who is absolutely incredible at finding historical stories that illustrate concepts for the emails that he writes. And these stories make tons of sales.

Sean showed me an email he wrote a while back. It told a story about how Frank "Lefty" Rosenthal (the inspiration for the movie *Casino*) was a world-renowned handicapper who could pick winners of sports bets with the precision of a brain surgeon.

He related this story about how some people seem to have a knack for picking winning Amazon products to create, list, and sell. And then he showed how the product could help you do the same. And this email crushed it, making over $15,000 in sales from a list of about 1,100 subscribers.

Stories work, plain and simple. Stories are super powerful. People will remember your stories; they're fodder to include for all sorts of different types of email campaigns that bring out your personality. It's very hard to leave your personality out of the stories told in your emails.

For a very simple way to implement this concept, think about your company: what were the happy experiences of all the clients or customers you've worked with? Tell a story every single day.

If you do that, and link to a product at the bottom of your email, or within the body copy of the email, you will make sales because people want to achieve the same results. It's a very simple strategy. The email on the following pages is a great example.

==================================

Subject: *I can't believe this guy...*

So this is pretty cool. I'm coaching this freelancer, and 7 weeks ago, when we started... he was brand spankin' new to the game.

Didn't have any paying copy clients... EVER.

He had some chops (I think he's got a lot of natural writing talent... lucky bastard. But to his credit... he also has a voracious appetite for copy knowledge).

I don't normally like taking on writers who are this wet behind the ears. I'll be honest with you... it's harder to get newbies results than it is for me to help a freelancer who's already got the ball rolling. If someone has already had a small handful of clients, it's super easy for me to teach them the ins and outs, and get 'em out there, talking with clients. But this guy was new. And I was a little unsure. I took him on anyway.

The first thing I did was send him my six-module Freelance Mindset Masterclass training program. It's a collection of six modules I filmed almost a year ago, which lays out all of the stuff I learned that helped me go from a dead broke school teacher to an in-demand freelancer within a few short years. It's mandatory that all my students go through this training before we ever hop on our first phone call. They need to internalize the principles and practices I teach in that course... it's designed to take them from 0-80% proficiency and understanding... and then we get to work on overcoming their other obstacles. (Most new freelancers have the same set of problems - no samples, no experience, no idea how to price, no ways to get clients, no idea how to sell on the phone, no confidence in themselves, no understanding of how to deal with clients, no understanding of HOW they should run their business and position themselves. This course solves ALL of that and gets people up to speed quick)

ANYWAY...

This guy watched the training.

We've hopped on 3 phone calls so far. It's only been 7 weeks since we started. Here's the email he just sent me...

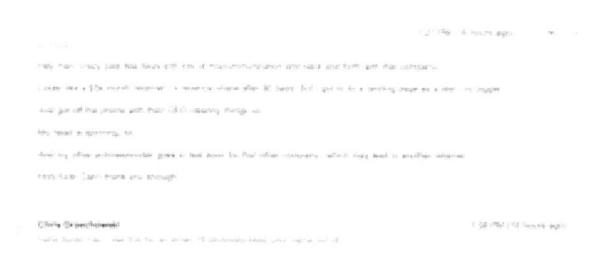

Look at this guy. He's got two retainers in 7 weeks... and one of 'em has a rev share/royalty options.

I gotta say... I am jealous. No joke.

Getting my first retainer took about 3 years. This guy's got two opportunities in less than 2 months. Now of course... he still has to close the deal here. Neither deal is inked yet. So relax...

The reason this guy has been able to achieve so much, so fast (in my opinion) is because he was already a hard worker and dedicated to making this happen. He just needed to learn how to actually land these kinds of deals.

So... that's what I taught him.

Pretty cool, huh?

Now...

> *If YOU want to learn how to get these kinds of opportunities... then you should join my upcoming coaching program with Kim Krause Schwalm.*
>
> *You get world-class LIVE training from two copywriters for the price of one. Well, not really for the price of one... it's MUCH more affordable than hiring either of us outright. I charge $500/hour for consults with business owners. Kim charges more. You're getting 3 live calls with both of us, plus Q&A... PLUS some bonuses I'm going to be announced in the next couple of days.*
>
> *And I promise you, each bonus will be worth more than this course itself. You shall see.*
>
> *You know what to do. Click this link: Click me!*
>
> *Secure your spot. Get training from Kim and me. Go forth and kick some serious but in your freelance career.*
>
> *See you there,*
>
> ***Chris Orzechowski***
>
> =================

It's simple. Tell a story, relate it to your product, and then insert the call to action.

Fourth Pillar: Smart Segmenting

One of the last big pillars is something I call smart segmenting. While you *can* get away with sending one email to every single person on your list, that's an inefficient and ineffective way to do things. There are so many easy ways to segment your list. For instance, there are ways to tag or exclude people from certain sequences, and include people in other promotions that help your deliverability, help the health of your list, and your relationship with the people on your list.

I have a course for freelancers about how to land retainers and loyalty deals. If someone buys that product, I won't continue to send them emails about buying that product, because they already own it. They won't buy that product twice.

If you have a consumable or a continuity product, then maybe that's okay, but it makes sense to segment your list and understand how to speak to each segment.

Within every list will be two (or more) different groups of people who have different needs. On my own email list, some people are copywriters while others are business owners. So those conversations with prospects will be two very different conversations. While doing a certain promotion, I don't know if I necessarily want to send the same emails to every single person on my list, because over time, that will ruin the health of the list.

Segmenting is super important.

As your business starts to grow, you will have many different segments.

Back in the day, there used to be a lot of list-based email service providers that would require you to manually move people onto a list or get them to opt-in to a new list, and then you would have to mail that list. Many of the newer email service providers use tags. It's really easy to tag people when they click a link or buy a product, or if they indicate interest in something. It's very easy to apply these tags to people, and then exclude people who have X tags and include people who have Y tags.

By segmenting your list, you can just send things that are relevant to people who want to hear from them. There is no easier way to kill a list than to send people stuff that doesn't interest them. Try and avoid that as much as possible.

Going back to the simple strategy, we will use all three campaigns interchangeably (autoresponder, broadcast, and launch). The overall objective is to move people from the prospect list (or tag) to the buyer list or tag. Once they buy our flagship product or our front-end product, we want to sell them the next product, whatever that might be. That's the way things naturally go. With every level of success reached by your clients or customers, there will always be new problems at that new level of success. What thing can you sell them on their journey, what's next? You can move them up your company's value ladder, or through your back end process, by putting them onto a buyer's list and segmenting them out from your main list.

Doing that will put you light years ahead of others; you'll see some real results. On my list are about 85 people who bought one of my copywriting products: my course on retainer and royalty deals. Instead of sending them more emails about the same product, I asked myself, *"What are the problems faced by these people on my list now that they've solve this first problem? How can I figure out a solution to their new problems?"*

Those conversations will be very different from the emails sent to everyone else, people who don't have that main product that I want them to buy.

I have worked with companies that segmented frequency and monetary value; we had a very big team with many implementers who could help us with all this stuff. Even though I don't think you need to get super crazy, almost everyone on your list should have some tags. You should know who these people are.

For a huge list, you don't have to manually tag every single person, but you can sort people with tags such as buyers and prospects, or even with tags for certain situations such as people who entered through a certain funnel, or people who have entered through a certain launch. Then you could start to look at the data. You could dive in and start to notice things.

For instance, I like to tag people when I do launches. For me and for some of my clients, within 20% to 40% of people who buy through a launch sequence, it's not the first launch they have experienced. Without tagging people, without keeping an eye on these metrics and that data, you won't know or gather those insights. You might think, *"Oh, well, I already did a promotion, and everyone on my list was willing to buy."*

I realized this a long time ago when I first launched a copywriting product to my very small list; I made 16 sales. I said, *"Oh, I guess that's everyone who wanted the product,"* and then two months later I relaunched it and made another 16 sales. Now I know that people need to go through a few email campaigns before they might be ready to buy.

That's the cool thing about this email strategy. As people go through your main autoresponder, some people will buy right then and there because they're ready. Move them out to the buyers' list and start them on that next level of support in your business.

Once Isn't Enough

If they don't buy immediately, they might buy through your broadcast sequence, so you can scoop up those other people. Some people need a lot longer timeframe before they are ready to make a decision. Some people have sat on my list for six months to a year before they bought anything, which is fine. Some people aren't as developed in their understanding of their problems. That's like a market awareness thing.

Eugene Schwartz talks about five levels of market awareness: unaware, problem aware, solution aware, product aware, and offer aware.

If someone's unaware, they don't even realize they have a problem. I don't know if a lot of people on your list will be at that level, because it depends on how they signed up for your list, but a certain segment will be unaware.

Some people don't even know they have a problem, while other people realize their life isn't as good as it can be, because they have a specific problem and there's a reason for it. Once they see they have a problem, they start searching for solutions and become solution aware. They start to realize something: *"To solve my problem, I can go with option A or B or C."* Once that happens, they become product aware, and they start to look at all of the products that can deliver those solutions.

If a person is overweight and they want to lose weight, they might realize there are a lot of different solutions. *"I could go keto or paleo, I could go vegetarian or Atkins, or maybe South Beach Diet."* Since there are different products they could buy, they say, *"Okay, there's keto program A, and keto program B, and book C and course D."* Once they reach the decision-making point, if they haven't bought, they might be waiting to take advantage of the right offer.

Since the people on your email list will go through those levels of awareness, it's good to have the combination of the autoresponders, the broadcast, and the launches. Some people who enter your funnel are very, very aware.

They know who you are and what you can do for them. They know what your products can do, and they want the result your products can deliver. They want your product. Those people will most likely buy into your front-end automated sequence.

Needs Change Over Time

For others, your broadcast series will warm them up over time. Through the content you deliver and the stories you tell, people will be brought up to their level of awareness. When I first started writing copy, I remember everyone talking about Seth Godin books, how great they were. I thought, *"I guess these are good, but I don't know how I could use this yet."*

Five years later, I was at a more developed point in my business and I started consuming everything he wrote. As I reached a higher level of awareness, I understood how those particular solutions could help me. In the beginning, the only thing I cared about was the copywriting stuff, but once I read enough of those books, I realized that I needed to learn other things in the business world.

As you send more and more emails over time, the 'buying resistance scale' begins to tip in your favor. On one side of the scale is the reason for buying, and on the other side is the buying resistance. The scale starts out even and balanced. If you start dropping little pebbles on the 'reason for buying' side, the scale tips in your favor. The pebbles are your emails. Every single email you send is another pebble.

The more pebbles you put onto your side of the scale, the more it tips in your favor. You've offered enough benefits and results, enough proof, to overcome enough objections through a combination of everything that you've done, so that people have enough reasons to buy.

Some people need deadlines to respond, and that's why the launches are good. As a writer, if I don't have a deadline for a project I'm working on, it won't get done. That shouldn't be the only way to sell something, because some people will only respond if and when they're ready. But you can sell a lot of these deadline-driven people when you have some launch or promotional events that include a deadline or consequence for not buying within a certain frame of time. You'll convert a lot of people that way, people who need to say, *"Okay, today's the last day I can get this thing or get these bonuses,"* or, *"Today's the last day I can get it for this price."*

Using stories and personality-based emails, you can move people through that system, get people onto your list, and build that initial bond through the autoresponder. You will be segmenting people as you go, adding them into your broadcast sequence, and then offering launches from time to time for different promotional offers.

The whole goal of this entire game, everything we do, is trying to move prospects onto the buyers' list. Once people become buyers, we ask, *"What's next? What would be the next solution that they need in their life, the next step on their journey?"* That next solution, whatever it is, that's the next offer you sell them.

Fifth Pillar: Your Central Theme

Because everyone is on a journey, that is the fifth pillar. You need to get clarity on the central theme that runs through your business and what you do, because everyone has certain goals in life, climbing their own personal Mount Everest. They are on your list because they think that you are the person who can help them move up the mountain. They are trying to get to the top and achieve that big goal; along the way are many, many milestones, so you need to determine the place on the mountain where you will be.

Will you be the person who drives them to the edge and gets them up to that first base camp, solving problems right at the beginning? Are your solutions a bit more in the middle of the mountain or closer to the top of the mountain, after they've solved all of those other problems?

Maybe you can guide someone up their entire mountain, from the beginning of their journey to the end. There are certain milestones on people's journeys where you will solve one problem for them, and then solve the next problem, and the next problem. You might be able to continue solving problems, or send them to someone else, or perhaps you'll need to develop new solutions that can continue to move people further and further up the mountain.

That central theme should go through all of your emails. *Get clarity on these people, who they are, their own personal journey, and all the benefits and results they want in life. How do your products match up with those? How can you demonstrate that with stories? What are their objections, and their reasons for not wanting to buy?* Next, think of stories that help overcome those objections.

You'll find yourself light years ahead in transforming your business, by using a combination of the five pillars. It is a little more nuanced than what we could include in this book, but if you start using the five pillars as a guide, you will start seeing pretty incredible results.

Working with Me

If you would like some help implementing these ideas into your own business, I work with people in many different ways. The main way will be to work with my agency, Orzy Media, where I partner with clients to help them get incredible results in their businesses, increasing revenue and profits. If you'd like to work with me, please go to **OrzyMedia.com** and fill out an application so we can talk.

If you want to see the emails we send out firsthand, you can join our email list. Once you submit your application to work with me, as we've done with many clients, I can partner with you to **"Make It Rain"** in your own business.

What I like to do is work with people long-term, helping them create effective campaigns that get incredible results in their business. We can do this a number of different ways: either through hiring my team and I to help you implement a better email strategy or through consulting and working together to create some of these campaigns that you or your team can implement.

Increase Amount of Sales That You're Currently Making from Your Email Marketing

It used to be easy to make money from email marketing, because everyone loved getting emails. They looked forward to all the cool messages in their inbox. You could get away with being lazy and just blasting out offers - people would buy all day.

The thing is, consumer behavior has evolved. In order to cut through the clutter and be that one brand people love buying from and develop a relationship with, you have to change your strategy. The best way to do that is with the strategies I show you in this book.

If you have found the information in this book to be valuable would like to work with me to implement the techniques in this book... so you can increase your revenue and profits from your email list, then:

Go to www.orzymedia.com and fill out an application to speak with me.

My team and I can consult with you and even create full email campaigns that can help find the money buried in your list.

There's a high chance you're leaving a lot of money on the table with an ineffective email marketing strategy. So if you'd like my team and I to help you fix this problem, contact us today.

Made in the USA
Coppell, TX
07 February 2022

73097604R10033